TO

ALFIE

LOVE FROM

Alfie

Alfie has a pet unlike any other. He doesn't have whiskers, or fur, or cute fluffy ears.

He doesn't fetch sticks in the park, or chase his tail, and he c curl up in Alfie's lap for a snooze.

But he does have three LITTLE toes.

And a L-O-N-G neck.

And an even L-O-N-G-E-R tail.

And that's because Alfie's pet is a dinosaur.

Called Dexter.

ıough Dexter can't meow, or bark, or squeak, or moo,
quack, he does have a great big roar. Just not today.

s ... gone," whispered Dexter. "Yesterday I was roaring
ds, but now there's nothing. Not even a growl."

can't have vanished completely," said Alfie.
e'll just have to look for it. Come on, let's go!"

l so their great roar hunt began....

First, Alfie and Dexter searched the park. As they walked around, Alfie thought he could hear something. Could it really be Dexter's roar?

OOMPAH! OOMPAH! OOMPAH

"That's not my roar, that's a brass band!" said Dexter.

"Carry on walking down the road," said the band leader. "I'm sure I heard something earlier today that could have been a roar."

"Thanks!" said Alfie. "Let's go, Dexter!"

TOOOOT
POM
POM
POM

ddenly, Alfie and Dexter heard a booming sound that got
der and louder.

the closer and closer they got, the less and less it sounded
a roar.

BOOM! BOOM! BOOM!

ie turned to Dexter: "That's not ..."

my roar," frowned Dexter.

a! My wrecking ball's never been mistaken for a dinosaur
r before," chuckled the crane driver. "Try the beach,
re's always strange noises coming from there."

"Phew," said Alfie. "All this roar hunting is tiring work. Come on, let's get an ice cream."

As Alfie and Dexter wandered across the sand they heard a distant sound getting closer.

"Uh-oh, what's that?" said Dexter.

SQUAWK! SQUAWK! SQUAWK!

"Aaahh! Seagulls!" shouted Alfie. "They're after the ice cream! Time for more roar hunting!"

FIRE

ran and ran and ran until they could run no more.

lenly, Dexter spotted something big, red and shiny coming
rds them. It was their friendly neighbourhood firefighters.

', our siren can make a noise as big as a roar," they said.
l that do?"

NEE-NAW! NEE-NAW! NEE-NAW!

m, it's kind of close, but it's still not really a roar," said Alfie.

a nee-no from me," said Dexter.

y don't you try asking a vet why your roar's disappeared?"
the firefighters. "We'll take you to see our friend – hop in!"

"I've never ever examined a dinosaur before," said the vet. "Oh well, here goes!"

"AAAHHH," said Dexter as she looked down his throat.

"EEEEK," said Dexter as she looked in his ears.

"WAA, that tickles," said Dexter as she examined his tummy.

"Well, this is strange, I can't see anything," puzzled the vet. "
don't you go to the school library and hunt for your roar there

CAT

BRRRRIIINNGGG
SCHOOL

ie spotted his best friend's brother in the playground.

inosaur books?" he said. "Yes, there's loads in the library.
in the main door and just follow the signs."

ome on, Dexter, let's go!" said Alfie.

HAT?" shouted Dexter.

e library!" explained Alfie.

HAT?!" yelled Dexter.

nblock your ears, Dexter!" said Alfie.

HAT?!?" bellowed Dexter.

And so the great roar hunt continued as they tiptoed into the library, trying their best not to be heard.

Alfie glanced back. "Whatever you do, Dexter, don't ..." *CLONK!* "... hit your head on the light shade. Or ..."

THUMP! THUMP! THUMP!

"... knock any books off the shelves. Or ..." *SSHHHH!* "... upset the librarian."

Alfie sighed. "Are you sure you're not a clumsy-saurus?!"

SHHH!
DICTIONARY
OF THE WORLD
QUIET PLEASE

D
DINO

y quickly found a comfy spot and started flicking through dinosaur books.

y luck?" asked Alfie.

ɔt yet," replied Dexter. "Oh wait, look!"

e peeked round excitedly.

ıink that's a picture of my Uncle Dave in this one!" ckled Dexter.

Book after book, page after page, they hunted and hunted u
Alfie noticed a big blue book tucked away in the corner.

"Hang on, that one's wobbling," said Alfie.

"What. Is. That?" said Dexter.

Alfie took a deep breath and opened it up. A ginormous roa
erupted from the pages and whooshed into Dexter's mouth.

"RRRROOOOOOAAAAAAARRRR!"

"YAAAAYYYY!" cheered Alfie.

"SHHHHHHH!" hissed the librarian.

"ROAR," whispered Dexter happily.

RRRRROOOOAARRRR

After a long day of brass band listening, seagull dodging, fire engine riding, puppy playing, library tiptoeing, head clon
and roar finding, Alfie and Dexter headed back home.

"What a roar-some day!" they cheered.

"Yay for roars and dino-snores," thought Alfie as he drifted o
to sleep and began to dream of his next BIG adventure....

Maybe I'll...
GO DIVING?

Alfie, look out for more **Mini Adventures** books.
Go to www.orangutanbooks.co.uk

Story by M.K. Scott
Illustrated by Jo Lindley
Designed by Ryan Dunn

orangutan

First published by Orangutan Books in 2019
Hometown World Ltd, 1 Queen Street, Bath BA1 1HE

Visit www.orangutanbooks.co.uk
Follow us @orangutanbooks

ISBN 978-1-78979-506-6

Printed in Italy
HTW_PO201929

FSC www.fsc.org
MIX
Paper from responsible sources
FSC® C023419